The Creative Flow Toolbox

Holistic Solutions for Writer's Block

A Creative Spirit Minibook

Alix Moore

Rising Moon Press
Clarksburg, Maryland

Rising Moon Press
24110 Clarksburg Road
Clarksburg, MD 20871
http://www.writerswithwings.com/

Author photo by Janice Jones
All other images © Istock
Book Layout © 2014 BookDesignTemplates.com
The Creative Flow Toolbox/Alix Moore
ISBN 978--0692413432

CONTENTS

What is Creative Flow?

Unite with the muse.
Write without stopping.
Know that your words are good.
Create!

A Journey into Creative Flow

Hello! I am so excited that you are here with me today to share in the profoundly joyous experience of creative flow. It's one of the most pleasurable and fulfilling experiences of my life, and I hope it will be of yours, as well.

As I write these words, it is a beautiful fall morning in Maryland. The sun is shining, the wind is shivering the changing leaves, and my roosters are talking to one another in the field outside my window. My feet are flat on the floor, my eyes are closed, and Pandora.com is set to one of my favorite creative channels—*Liquid Mind.*

There are many things I love about my life here on Rising Moon Farm, and the dog resting at my feet is one of them. So is the woman still sleeping at the other end of the house, and the horse sunbathing in front of the barn at the bottom of the hill. I am grateful to have all of these beings in my life.

And I am deeply grateful to have learned about creative flow, and to be able to descend at will into the communion it represents. This experience has transformed my life, and it's something I want you to be able to experience, as well.

Creative flow is the perfect antidote to writer's block. Flow produces the best writing you have ever done. The state of flow is a state of connection to your inner genius—your divine self. It's a quiet place that allows you to hear the voice of your intuition and the guidance of your angels. You can sink into flow to write, or to receive guidance to support you as you walk your author's path. Best of all, flow *feels* wonderful. It's relaxing, invigorating, full of joy.

What is Creative Flow?

So, what *is* creative flow?

Have you ever been driving down the highway, walking the dog, or taking a shower when words began to fill your head? Perhaps the first lines of a poem floated into your consciousness, or the solution to a plot problem was suddenly clear.

Can you recall a writing session when your words seemed to write themselves? Perhaps your characters took charge and wrote their own dialog, or you were so immersed in what you were typing that hours went by and you hardly noticed?

Creative flow is a state of being in the zone, just as athletes are in the zone. Your mind stills, your body relaxes, and everything about you is focused and subsumed into the act of writing.

Wouldn't you like to be able to visit this state of effortless creativity every time you sit down to write? Not only is this possible—it's essential. For it's during flow that we write our most important words. Our deepest truths, our most lighthearted scenes, our most believable characters—they all come during these moments, when the critical, evaluative voice inside our head is turned off and the words come from deep within us.

I know this state well. During times of flow, I am the garden hose, and the words flow through me like water. I want you to know what I know, to be able to write without baggage or block, in joyous communion with your highest creative self. We all have a genius within, whether you call it your divine self, your intuition, or your Muse. If we tap into that inner genius, we can let the words write us: in joy, without effort—in the flow.

Flow requires that all the aspects of our selves are balanced and unified. Emotions, body, mind, and ego all must settle, become still, align. With this four-way balance, we make a home for our spirits, our genius selves.

Yet most of us do not live in this state of balance. One aspect of our personality usually takes over, while other aspects recede. When that happens, the synergy of the whole is disrupted, flow stops, and writing becomes effortful.

Let's explore what happens when one aspect or another of your personality dominates the creative union. Notice which examples of disunity resonate with you.

Overwhelming Emotions

An emotionally sensitive person may experience
- Frequent mood swings
- Empathy with the emotions of others
- Anger
- Depression
- Despair
- Guilt
- Righteous indignation

Writers who are very sensitive to emotions may find that negative emotions fill their bodies and thoughts to the exclusion of the quiet emptiness their creativity needs.

These writers can spend a lot of energy feeling discouraged, depressed, or resentful. They may feel as if they aren't getting the recognition they deserve or the response they are looking for, or they may feel overwhelmed by a sense of inadequacy or hopelessness.

Some people are very sensitive to the emotions of others, and they may find themselves strongly affected by the anger or depression of family members, friends, or colleagues. All these negative emotions affect our stability, our neutrality, and our ability to connect to the genius within.

If this sounds like you, check out the **Happiness Toolbox.**

A Depleted Physical Body

Your physical body may need your attention if

- You never seem to have the energy to do what you want to do
- You are struggling with chronic or frequent illness
- You are chronically sleep deprived
- You rarely eat nourishing whole foods
- You're jittery or hyperactive

Writers with depleted physical bodies may complain of not being able to find the energy to write. On a night when they finally set aside time to be creative, they may find it hard to turn off the television and get off the couch.

Writing takes tremendous energy, even though it's not a very physically demanding activity. If you are responsible for caring for children or aging parents, or if you have a very demanding job, you may find your creative well running dry because your physical body needs care.

If this sounds like you, check out the **Renewal Toolbox.**

A Dominant Mind

An overactive mind is

- Judgmental
- Logical
- Planning
- Churning

- Doubting
- Busy busy busy!

If you tend to live in your mind, you may find that the voices inside your head are rarely silent. You may think your way through life, and find yourself reluctant to rely on the advice of your intuition. In fact, you may actively use logic to discredit your intuition, only to find out later that your wise self was right.

When it comes time to write, you may find that writing is challenging. You may revise often, feel critical of your work, or have trouble getting started.

You may find it hard to meditate, as your mind continues to evaluate, plan, and question everything. You may float from project to project without a clear sense of direction and without completing tasks.

If this sounds like you, check out the **Serenity Toolbox.**

An Overactive Ego

A writer with an overactive ego often
- Lives in future time
- Daydreams about fame, recognition, and success
- Spends more time daydreaming than taking action
- Feels a sense of entitlement or superiority
- Feels a sense of inadequacy or failure
- Worries about rejection or piracy
- Tries to control uncontrollable things

Ego energy and creative flow can't exist at the same time, so if you are continually thinking about what your writing will bring you in terms of money or fame, it's likely that your authentic creativity is suffering.

If you are consumed with the necessity of making money from your writing, or if you are terrified to share your work with the world, check out the **Self-Esteem Toolbox.**

A Disconnected Spirit

Your spirit, or inner genius, brings the power of your divine self into everyday life, smoothing the way to your goals. However, many people aren't consciously connected to their higher selves.

A writer with a disconnected spirit

- Often feels powerless
- Faces challenges that feel insurmountable
- Rarely asks Source energy for guidance and support
- Struggles to connect with the voice of intuition
- May struggle to define a passion and purpose
- May be unclear about the benefits his or her books bring to readers
- Would like more joy and serenity but isn't sure how to achieve it

If this sounds like you, check out the **Divinity Toolbox.**

Finding Flow

The goal of this book is to help you find creative flow, now and anytime you choose. To do that, I have created a toolbox full of exercises to rebalance each of the four aspects of your unified self, plus some very powerful tools that will help you connect with your higher self. All the tools promote unity and flow. Pay attention to which tools interest you—start anywhere, and follow your inner wisdom as you use the material in this book. There is no wrong way to use this book.

The key word is *use*, however. You can't just read; you must take action for the exercises to work. If you use the tools, you will find that your writing practice changes and deepens. You will tap into your source of effortless creativity and your words will be unstoppable, and bright.

The Happiness Toolbox: For Emotional Balance

Release negative emotions.
Have faith.
Choose gratitude.
Breathe!

Honor the Fear

Is there something on your writer's to-do list that you're afraid to do?

First, honor the fear. Our fear always contains wisdom—information about where we need to grow. Write down at least three reasons why taking that step feels risky to you. Don't judge the reasons—just list them. Sit quietly with your fear and be open to any insights that arise. How does the fear change when you accept it instead of trying to minimize it?

Cultivate Solitude

Creativity requires time alone. All too often, we allow our lives to fill with noise, people, or responsibilities. However, we also have a responsibility to ourselves, and we need to honor our own need for space and solitude.

Build in time alone, every day if possible, and model great self-care for your family. If you respect your alone time, everyone else will, too.

Breathe Your Way to Calmness

Sit or stand, with both feet flat on the floor. Breathe normally. Each time you inhale, think "I am." And each time you exhale, think "calm." Repeat these words in time with your breathing for ten breaths. If you practice this, eventually you will be able to access your calmness with just one or two breaths.

Throw Out the TV

Television is huge time waster, and it trains our minds to receive instead of create. Here are five reasons to get rid of your television:

You'll spend more time reading.

You'll spend more time writing.

You'll reduce the amount of negativity in your life.

You'll feel less fear.

You'll actually experience life instead of just viewing it.

Blow Bubbles

Bubbles are a great way to get rid of anger, fear, frustration, or any other unwanted emotion.

With your feet flat on the floor and your eyes closed, imagine a huge shimmering bubble out in front of you. Begin to dump fear into the bubble. See it flowing out of you and filling up the bubble in front of you. You can also dump impatience, envy, frustration, rejection, or any negative emotion that you want to dump.

Fill up the bubble until it can't hold any more; then send it off to the edge of the universe and blow it up. Don't forget this step—it doesn't do much good to fill up bubbles and leave them hanging around in your energy space!

Get another bubble, and repeat the whole procedure until you send the last one off.

~From *Writer, the World Needs You: Get Past Your Fear and Write the Words You're Meant to Write!*

Be Grateful in Your Bones

So many teachers talk about gratitude and the way it can change your life. But there's a catch—being grateful in your mind won't suffice. Gratitude is powerful only when we fully embody it, when we are grateful all the way down in our bones. So think of just one thing, one thing that you are so grateful for that you feel it all the way down in your bones. Spend a few minutes each day being truly grateful for that one thing.

Take an Opening Breath

Breathe in through your nose and exhale through your mouth with the soft sound of "ahhhhh."

This is the opening breathe. It invites our spirits to settle more fully in our bodies, and connect us with our deep intuitive knowing.

At the beginning of a writing session, or whenever you feel stuck, take one or more opening breaths. Ahhhhh.

The Renewal Toolbox: For Physical Balance

Honor the needs of the body.
Prioritize beauty.
Keep the creative well full.
Ground yourself!

Surround Yourself with Beauty

Spirit craves beauty.

First, then, create order and beauty around the writing space. I write from a studio tucked away on the viewless side of the house. I don't see the mountains from my windows or the storms rolling in across the valley. I do see chickens at eye level as they scratch in the mulch outside my screen.

The dog comes by my window when he wants in. Bending down to peer at me, he requests that I pause in the midst of inspiration and rise, and let him in.

My beauty is chickens and the beloved ears of my king shepherd and the trails of pothos down the bookshelf. My beauty is the found things, antlers and deer skulls that watch over me, like muses.

What is your beauty? Fill your space with your beauty, not mine. Create a place that fills you, and that will be a place where you can write.

From *Tapping the Well Within: Writing from Your Source of Effortless Creativity, Deep Wisdom, and Utter Joy.*

Sleep

It's impossible to create at a high level when your body is exhausted. Chronic sleep deprivation limits your creative potential. Reprioritize your life so that you get enough sleep. Nap often!

Say No!

Just say no.
> Practice disappointing others.
> Clear your life of the unimportant.
> Prioritize your art.

Prioritize Your Energy

Your potential is limitless, but your creative energy is not. Are you spending your energy on what you think is most important, or are you just operating on guilt, responsibility, and habit? Start choosing carefully where you spend your time and energy, so that you have plenty left to write with.

Ground Yourself—Feet on Earth

Grounding ourselves renews our energy and restores wellness to our physical bodies. Research shows that spending time with our bare feet in contact with the earth has numerous health benefits. A fast way to ground yourself is to go outside and sit or walk in bare feet on dirt or grass or sand.

Visit Dr. Mercola's website, www.mercola.com, to read more about this technique and the science behind it.

Declutter

Cluttered rooms trap and hold energy, resulting in energetic sludge that operates like dirt. Past times and past emotions get stuck in corners and crevices. These stuck energies weigh us down and can keep us trapped in old patterns. Spring-clean your energy by cleaning and decluttering your space—starting with your writing studio.

Fill the Creative Well

The well of spirit within is just like any other well. As water or inspiration flows out, water and inspiration must also flow in, or the well will run dry. Each of us is different; so what refills the well of Spirit will also be different for each of us. I invite you to remember what feeds *your* spirit. And then, after you remember what you love to do, I invite you to give yourself permission to do it.

From *Tapping the Well Within: Writing from Your Source of Effortless Creativity, Deep Wisdom, and Utter Joy.*

The Serenity Toolbox: For Mental Balance

Affirm peace.
Love yourself.
Get into your body.
Move!

Move!

To get out of your mind, you need to get into your body!

Movement can be as simple as walking down the driveway to get the mail, or as sophisticated as learning to tango or belly dance. Ride a horse, sail a boat, ice skate, swim—however you like to move, make sure you *do* move. Every day. Rhythmic, routine movement is like compost for your imagination.

Unplug

"Hello? It's god calling."

"I'll be right with you, just let me answer this email."

Electronic noise fills up the creative space with clutter. When you are constantly reading email, listening to music or news, or watching television, your own creativity can't compete. For part of each day, unplug it all. (Yes, sigh, you *can* set a timer to tell you when it's time to plug it all back in!)

Eat Well

The Standard American Diet is "S.A.D." Garbage in, as they say, is garbage out. What you feed your body directly affects the way it can serve you.

Don't worry about eliminating unhealthy foods. Instead, focus on adding one or more healthy foods to your life. The more you focus on increasing healthful food, the more your diet will change, effortlessly. Eventually you will lose interest in the junk food you used to crave.

Take a Shower; Go For a Walk

Feeling stuck? The very best thing you can do is to grab the dog and go for a walk. It gets you outdoors into nature with your animal companion, which is great for creative renewal.

I often work for several hours in the morning, following up by talking a shower or walking my dog. Invariably, I end up with new insights, back in the flow.

Practice Affirmations

Our minds chatter all day long. Give your mind something positive to focus on. Replace your negative self-talk with positive statements such as these:

I find readers effortlessly.

My income is constantly increasing.

My words bring healing and hope to my readers and the planet.

Affirmations reflect goals that we are reaching for—but they're written as if the goal has already come true. Put your affirmations on index cards around your house and say them often.

Love Your Work

So much of the artist's journey is grounded in fear: *Will I make it? Am I good enough?* To balance that fear, you need to fall in love with your own work. Curl up somewhere cozy with a cup of tea and your writing. Reread your words, and just love them. Wallow in gratitude for this amazing gift of your own amazing spirit. Wow!

Write with Your Eyes Closed

Sit in a comfortable place with your feet flat on the floor and your computer or notepad before you. Allow your attention to sink into your feet, until you can feel your feet fully connect with the floor. Breathe. Send a beam of light from the top of your head up to the heavens. Feel your crown opening like a flower of light. Rest quietly and feel the connection down to earth and up to sky. When the words come, do not judge them. Simply write—with your eyes closed. (Yes, you can peek occasionally to make sure your fingers are on the right keys.) This works especially well during or after meditation.

Take a Meditative Walk

Go for a walk and, at first, concentrate only on what you hear. What noises are near you? Far away? Spend several minutes walking with your attention on what is audible. Then concentrate only on what you can see. Next, focus on how your body feels, then on what you smell, and finally on what you feel emotionally. End with all your senses in balance.

The Self-Esteem Toolbox: For Ego Balance

Let go of the reins.
Let go of the fear.
Surrender.
Trust!

Clean House!

But wait! I'm a great writer here! What do you mean—clean my house?

Yup. It's an ego thing. Go scrub your bathroom, and while you're at it, declutter your living room. Your creative spirit needs space and beauty to work in, and your ego needs—some time with a scrub brush.

Play

It's impossible to be in your ego when you are playing. Children and animals are especially good playmates, as they are rarely in their egos.

Find a friend or two and do something for no other reason than pure enjoyment. Pleasure, laughter, fun—they all fill the creative well. Make a list of ten ways you like to play, then pick one and do it.

Accept & Allow

Release impatience and self-judgment. Breathe.

Close your eyes and imagine that you inhale acceptance and exhale pushing, forcing, and making things happen. Allow yourself to be where you are in this exact minute. You're on the path. You're doing fine.

Rest in the peace of this understanding.

Look in the Mirror

Pick up a small hand mirror or stand in front of the bathroom mirror. Make eye contact with yourself, and tell yourself that you are loved and that your writing is worthwhile.

> *I love you. You are a fabulous writer, and the world needs your words.*

Use your own words to affirm your self-love and the value of your work. Repeat daily until you believe it's true.

Thanks to Louise Hay for this powerful exercise.

Surrender

Like gratitude, this is another thing we have to learn in our bones. When life is full of challenges and your goal seems impossible to achieve, just surrender and turn the whole thing over to the divine. Ask for help, release control. We can't *make* anything happen. Let go and let god.

Phew! What a relief!

Take the Next Baby Step

Do you have a goal or a dream for your creative journey? If the road to your dream seems impossibly long, scary, or confusing, the very best advice is just to take one tiny baby step.

You don't have to get from here to your goal; you just need to take the next step. What's the next tiny thing you can do?

Just do it—and then do the next tiny thing. It's easier than you think.

Ask the Fear Question

Fear is one of the biggest stumbling blocks on the road to success. Often we feel stuck or we hesitate to take action because, at some unconscious level, we are afraid. Here's a great tool to see how fear is holding you back.

Place your hand on your heart and say out loud, "If I weren't afraid . . . " and finish the sentence without hesitating. Don't overthink it. What did you learn?

Thanks to Sonia Choquette for this powerful exercise.

Go with the Energy Flow

Most writers have half a dozen projects in progress at any one time. It's easy to feel scattered and unsure of what to do with your time. Sometimes, too, we start a project but we need to let it rest for a while before we are ready to finish it. If you're not sure which writing project to work on, notice where you feel the most energy and excitement. Then go with the flow, and work on that project.

Thanks to Christine Agro for this helpful concept.

The Divinity Toolbox: For Spiritual Balance

Choose to heal yourself and the planet.
Accept your own power.
Take baby steps.
Grow!

Ground Yourself and Meditate

Grounding meditation is the most powerful tool I know for learning to access creative flow, because it connects you directly with your higher self. Here are the basic steps:

Sit in a comfortable seat with your feet flat on the floor. Close your eyes. With your imagination, pick a color of light, and attach a tube of light in that color to the base of your spine. Let the tube of light extend down through your body, through your chair, and down through the building that you are in, until it reaches the center of the earth. Attach the tube of light securely to the center of the earth.

Allow the tube of light to expand until it is as big around as your physical body. It should be as wide at the bottom as it is at the top. This tube of light is called a grounding cord, and it connects you with the planet.

On the tube of light there is a release switch. Turn it on, and allow all the energy that no longer serves you to flow down the grounding cord (your light tube) until it reaches the center of the earth, where it can be recycled. You don't need to identify the energy you are releasing; just set your intention to clear out anything that it's not in your best interest to carry. Release anything that is blocking your path. Sit like this for ten to twenty minutes, or as long as you like. Don't worry about anything your mind does during this time. It doesn't matter.

For more on this technique, see *Tapping the Well Within: Writing from Your Source of Effortless Creativity, Deep Wisdom, and Utter Joy.*

Pick a Daily Spiritual Practice

Choosing and sustaining a daily spiritual practice will go a long way toward connecting you with your creative spirit and enhancing creative flow. I use the grounding meditation on the previous page, but you can use whatever works for you.

There are many styles of yoga, of meditation, and of prayer. Experiment until you find something that you love. Commit to spending at least twenty minutes each day in connection with Source energy.

Choose

In order to grow, you must choose to grow.

Growth is not an easy road, but it is tremendously worthwhile.

Choose to step into your powerful self.

Choose to share your gifts with the world.

Ask for Help

We don't have to do this alone!

Our spirit guides, the angels, and the divine are always there, just waiting for us to ask for help.

Your intuition is also there, ready with guidance for you. Ask for help—you'll be amazed at the response you get.

Divine Timing

Wondering why you're not yet an overnight success? Things happen when it's time for them to happen. If you're not a rock star—yet—then it may be because that level of fame would completely crash your servers.

Trust that things happen when the time is right, and be grateful for the protection that brings. You need time to grow into success.

The Journey
Continues . . .

Embrace change.
Be peaceful.
Embody the muse.
Connect!

About Alix

My Spirit Says

My spirit says that I am
Here to be light, that I am
Here to be fearless,
Here to be an example.
My spirit says all is well.
My spirit says, teach peace,
Teach empowerment, teach the
Tools of living as a divine spark
Inside a human body.
Breathe.

Hi, I'm Alix.

I'm a writer, speaker, and teacher. I help writers connect with their creative spirits and transcend their fear so that they can create and market their writing with confidence and joy.

Life as a writer challenges us to grow into the people we were meant to be, but we don't have to do it the hard way.

We can use metaphysical tools that get us out of our minds and into our powerful, intuitive selves.

It's my passion to support writers because I believe that creativity is a tremendously healing force for each of us individually, as well as for our planet and the collective consciousness.

When I'm not writing or presenting workshops, you can find me raising chickens, training cows, or napping on my organic farm, in Clarksburg, MD.

Books by Alix

The Abundance Diet for Writers
The Creative Flow Toolbox: *Holistic Solutions for Writer's Block*
Full Moon, New Earth: *Poems of Joy for the Collective Journey*
The Gift: *How My Horse Taught Me to Teach the Toughest Children*
Tapping the Well Within: *Writing from Your Source of Effortless Creativity, Deep Wisdom, and Utter Joy*
Writer, the World Needs You: *Get Past Your Fear and Write the Words You're Meant to Write*

Contact Alix

Email: alix@writerswithwings.com
Website: http://www.writerswithwings.com
Social media
    Twitter: @AuthorAlixMoore
    Facebook: WriterswithWings

Dear Reader,

Thank You!

I'm grateful that you've traveled with me through these pages. I hope these tools support your creative journey.

In case you haven't figured it out, it's my passion to help others connect with their powerful, peaceful, divinely creative selves.

I invite you to drop by my website, writerswithwings.com, and check out the resources I have gathered there to support your creativity.

I'd love to hear from you about how your creativity is blossoming or about the blocks you are overcoming. Please feel free to drop me an email at alix@writerswithwings.com.

In joy,
Alix

Read On!

Agro, Christine,
    www. christineagro.com/.com.
Choquette, Sonia,
    http://soniachoquette.com.
Hay, Louise
    http://www.louisehay.com.
Mercola, Joseph,
    http://www.mercola.com.